CATCH A CRICKET
by
Carla Stevens
Illustrated by Martin Iger

Do you like to dig for worms? If you find one, put it in a jar and watch him tunnel through the earth, and then put him back in the garden where he is needed. In the nighttime, try to catch a firefly. They aren't easy to catch, but they are fun to watch in a jar by your bed when their lights blink on and off. Then, CATCH A CRICKET! Put him in a jar with holes punched in it and then listen to him *chiiirrruuup*. He makes this friendly noise with his wings. A grasshopper is different and must be fed and given water every day, if you put him in a jar. He makes a singing noise by rubbing his legs and wings together. He'll jump away from you in a hurry if you give him a chance. Another funny little creature you can enjoy is a caterpillar. He's soft and woolly and will crawl up your arm. When winter comes it is harder to find things to catch, but save some jars and next spring and summer you can go catching again!

K

Classification and Dewey Decimal: Insects (595.7)

About the Author:

Recalling her own childhood habit of collecting and keeping insects in bureau drawers and noting her children's similar tendencies, CARLA STEVENS decided there must be a better way for other children to get to know worms and insects. She began to collect glass jars for the insects her children caught and material for her book. Mrs. Stevens is a graduate of New York University. She taught school in New York City before her marraige to Leon Stevens, a freelance writer. The Stevens family now live in a small Connecticut town.

About the Illustrator:

MARTIN IGER has taken pictures on land, under water and in the air. From his own plane he has taken aerial shots of islands, bridges and flying circuses. As a skin diver he photographed a submarine under water and a championship water polo game.

catch a cricket

ABOUT THE CAPTURE AND CARE OF CRICKETS, GRASSHOPPERS, FIREFLIES, AND OTHER COMPANIONABLE CREATURES

BY CARLA STEVENS / PHOTOS BY MARTIN IGER

1967 FIRST CADMUS EDITION
THIS SPECIAL EDITION IS PUBLISHED BY ARRANGEMENT WITH
THE PUBLISHERS OF THE REGULAR EDITION
WILLIAM R. SCOTT, INC.
BY
E. M. HALE AND COMPANY
EAU CLAIRE, WISCONSIN

This edition lithographed in U.S.A. by Wetzel Brothers, Inc., Milwaukee, Wisconsin

2B-9197

2B- 91

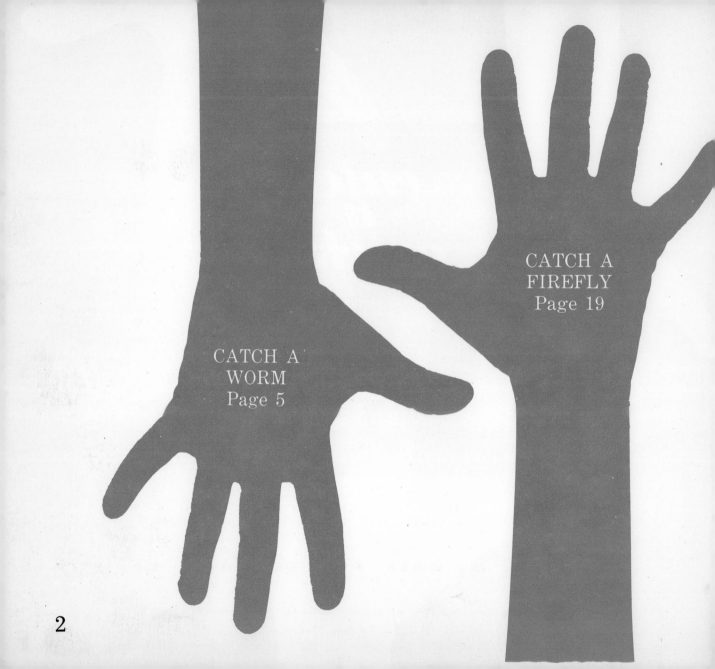

CATCH A
WORM
Page 5

CATCH A
FIREFLY
Page 19

2

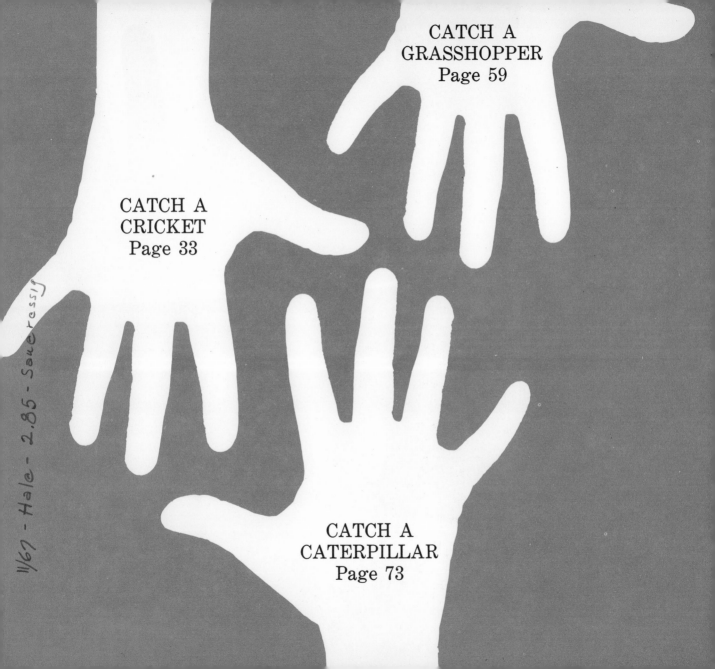

CATCH A
GRASSHOPPER
Page 59

CATCH A
CRICKET
Page 33

CATCH A
CATERPILLAR
Page 73

11/67 - Hale - 2.85 - Saueressig

4

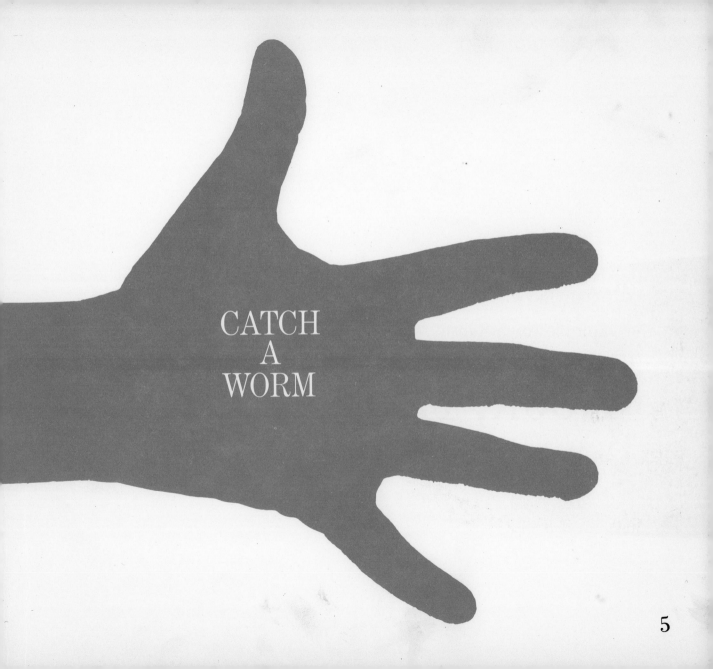

CATCH
A
WORM

Do you like to dig in the soft earth?
You find lots of things when you dig—
worms, for instance.

Look, there's a worm!

Do you want to keep him for a little while?

Let your worm stay on the ground near you
while you put some soft earth in a glass jar.

9

Where is your head, Mr. Worm?

It's hard to find a worm's head

because he has no nose or eyes.

He has a mouth, though,

a mouth so small

you can't really see it.

He needs a mouth so that he can eat.

The earth has old pieces of leaves

and plants in it.

Good things for a worm to eat!

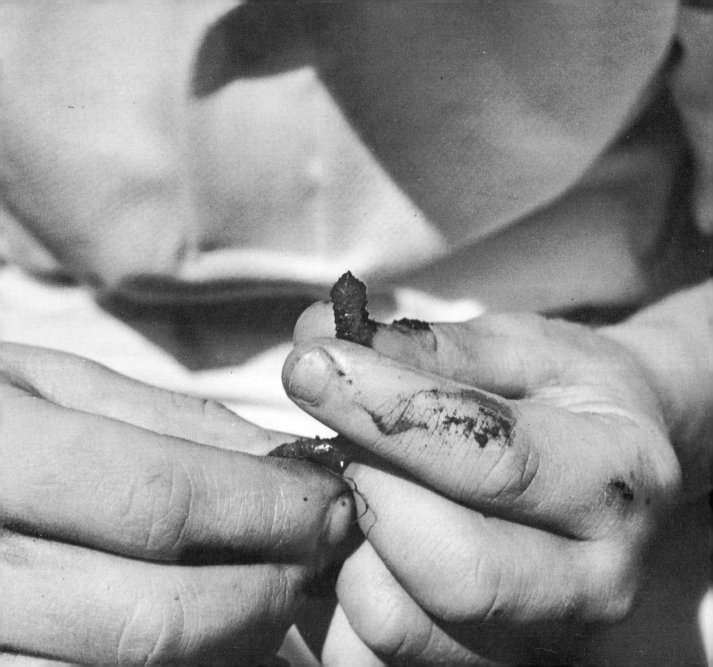

When you put your worm in the jar,
don't be surprised if he disappears.
He has probably tunneled his way
into the earth.

The worm moves along underground,
eating the earth in front of him.
As he moves, he leaves a tunnel.
See the tunnel your earthworm has made?

When they make their tunnels,
worms help your plants to grow faster, too.
As worms crawl along underground,
they loosen the earth around the plants
so that air and rain can get to the plant roots
more easily.
Look at the earth near the top of your jar.
Do you see those lumpy bits of soil?
Those lumps are the earth
your worm has swallowed,
digested, and gotten rid of.
They are called castings.
The castings that worms leave
make very good soil for your garden.

That's why you should put your worm outside again
when you don't want him any more.

Dig a little hole for him
in the soft ground and cover him gently.
Your garden needs him.

CATCH
A
FIREFLY

Early in the summertime,
when it begins to get dark,
you can see the lights of tiny fireflies
from your window.
Would you like to catch some of those fireflies?
Put some grass into a large glass jar.
Ask your mother to punch a few holes in the cover.
Then, take your jar outside
and set it down beside you.

There!

Do you see that tiny green light shining on the grass?

That's a firefly.

It won't be too hard to catch,

if it doesn't fly away.

Slowly, slowly,

go over to the light.

Now close your hands over the light like this.

Peek inside your hands.
Do you see a little light?
You do?
You have caught a firefly!
Put your hands over the jar,
drop your firefly inside,
and put the cover on.

Why don't you catch another firefly?
When you have two or three in your jar,
you will have more lights to watch.

See the white part of his tail?
That's where your firefly's light comes from.
Those two long feelers
sticking out of his head
are antennae.
The firefly uses his antennae
to feel around for a safe place to walk.

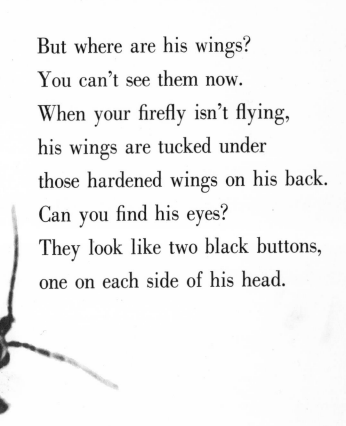

But where are his wings?
You can't see them now.
When your firefly isn't flying,
his wings are tucked under
those hardened wings on his back.
Can you find his eyes?
They look like two black buttons,
one on each side of his head.

When it is time to go to bed,
put your fireflies on a table near you.
You can watch the little lights
blink on and off, on and off,
on and off,
until you fall asleep.

Fireflies don't live a long time
even out of doors,
so don't expect to keep them
for more than a few days.
Don't worry about feeding them, either.
Some people say they eat tiny insects,
and others say they don't eat anything at all.
If you miss the lights of your little fireflies
when they die,
you can always go out
and catch some more.

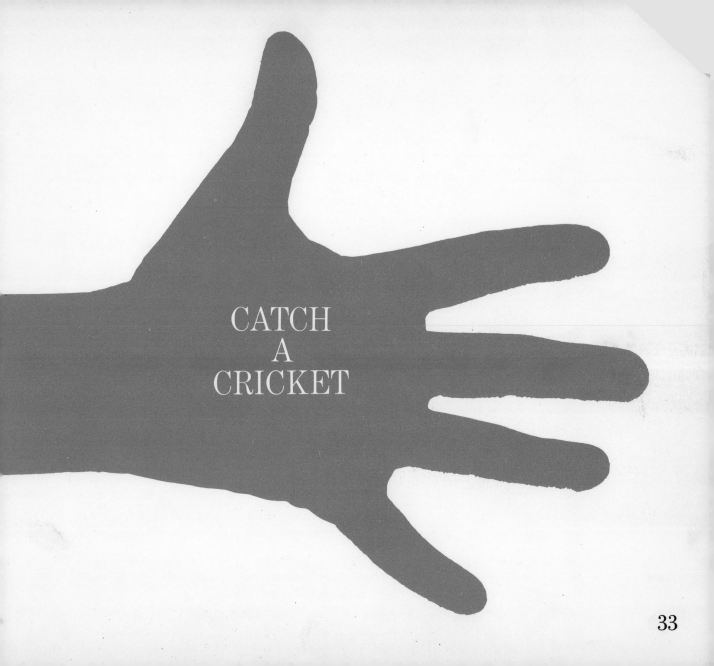

CATCH
A
CRICKET

33

Would you like a chirping noise
to sing you to sleep?
If you catch a cricket and put him in a glass jar,
with a little dirt and grass at the bottom,
he will chirp for you.
Listen!
Do you hear a chirping noise?
Where is it coming from?

Crickets hide under rocks.
Lift up that flat rock
and see if a cricket is hiding there.

38

QUICK
CATCH
HIM!

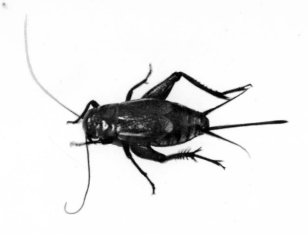

Does your cricket have a long spike on its tail?
That's a mother cricket.
She lays her eggs in the ground
with her long spike.
She doesn't make any chirping noises at all.
So put her back and start looking
for the cricket that you heard.

there's one

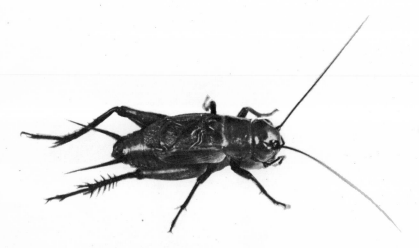

It doesn't have a spike on its tail.

It must be a chirping cricket.

Oh-h-h-h! He tickles!

He jumps too.
If you want to keep him,
put him in your jar
and put a cover on top.
Be sure the cover has some holes in it —
your cricket needs air.

Crickets eat roots, seeds, and berries
that grow on the ground.
You can feed your cricket
bread crumbs, raisins, and bits of lettuce.
Just one raisin and two bread crumbs
and a tiny piece of lettuce, though.
Your cricket is small,
so that's a lot of food for him.

Your cricket needs water to drink, too.
Wet your fingers and shake them
just above the jar.
The water that goes into the jar
will look like little raindrops —
raindrops for your cricket to drink
when he is thirsty.

CHIIIIRRRUUUP

CHIIIIRRRUUUP, CHIIIIRRRUUUP

CHIIIIRRRUUUP

CHIIIIRRRUUUP, CHIIIIRRRUUUP

CHIIIIRRRUUUP

CHIIIIRRRUUUP, CHIIIIRRRUUUP

CHIIIIRRRUUUP

CHIIIIRRRUUUP

CHIIIIRRRUUUP, CHIIIIRRRUUUP

CHIIIIRRRUUUP

CHIIIIRRRUUUP

CHIIIIRRRUUUP, CHIIIIRRRUUUP

CHIIIIRRRUUUP

CHIIIIRRRUUUP, CHIIIIRRRUUUP

CHIIIIRRRUUUP, CHIIIIRRRUUUP.

CHIIIIRRRUUUP, CHIIIIRRRUUUP

CHIIIIRRRUUUP

CHIIIIRRRUUUP, CHIIIIRRRUUUP

CHIIIIRRRUUUP, CHIIIIRRRUUUP

Chiiiirrruup, chiiiirrruuup.
How does a cricket make that
chirping noise?
He makes that noise
with his wings —
He scrapes one wing across
the edge of the other.
Chiiiirrruuup, chiiiirrruuup.

What is he feeling for with his long antennae?
Maybe he's trying to get out of the jar.

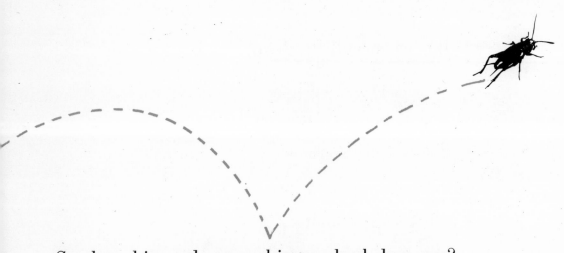

See how big and strong his two back legs are?

They are his jumping legs.

You'll find out what a good jumper he is

if you forget to put the cover back on your jar!

But when will he chirp?

You may have to wait until you go to bed
and it is dark and you are very quiet.
Then he will sing —
and sing each night
until the summer is over
and he dies,
or until you are tired
of that chirping noise in your room
and you put him outside again
near the flat rock where you found him.

58

CATCH
A
GRASSHOPPER

Where are you going with that big jar?

What are you looking for
in the tall, tickly grass?
You're putting something in the jar.
What is it?

A grasshopper!
Tap your jar a bit and
watch him jump.
What strong legs he has.
No wonder he can jump so high.
He jumps with those legs
and he makes noises with them, too.
When a grasshopper rubs his
legs and wings together, he makes
a singing noise.

You can see his two large eyes.
But he has three more eyes
on the top of his head —
they are not so easy to find.
How would you like to have
five eyes like a grasshopper?

Hey there, Mr. Grasshopper!
What are you eating?
Grass, of course.

Feed your grasshopper every day.
His appetite is very big, and
he eats almost anything.
You might try feeding him
different kinds of foods
to see what he likes best —
bread crumbs, dry cereal, bits of fruit.
Don't forget to give him a drink, too.
Wet your fingers and sprinkle
some water into the jar.
When you don't want to bother
feeding your grasshopper any more,
take him outside and put him on the ground.

There he goes —
jump, jump, jumping
away in the grass.

Good-by, Mr. Grasshopper

CATCH
A
CATERPILLAR

73

Would you like to have
a "woolly bear" in your room?
I'm just teasing you.
Not a real bear, of course.
I mean a "woolly bear" caterpillar.
If you take a walk
on a country road in the fall,
you'll probably find one crawling along.

See that black spot on the road?
That must be a "woolly bear" caterpillar.

Put your hand on the ground near the caterpillar
and he will crawl up on to your fingers.

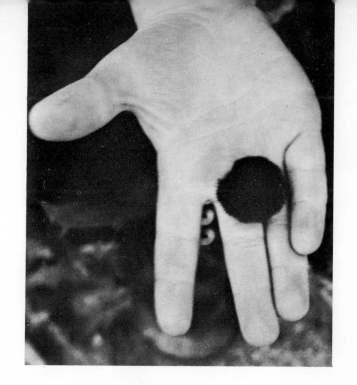

Oh look, he has curled himself into a little ball.
Is he dead?
No. He is playing dead
so that you'll put him down.
Stroke his furry body gently.
Your little caterpillar will crawl again
when he is not afraid.

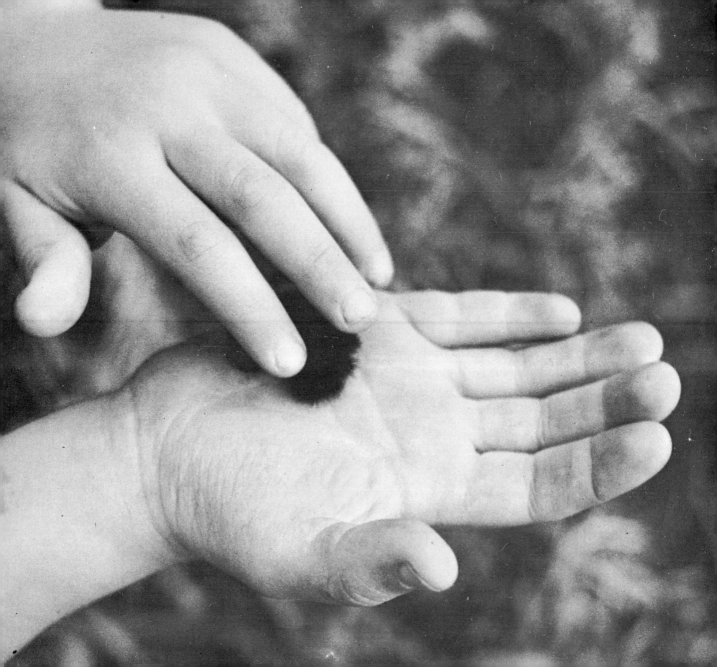

There he goes!

Where are you going, furry caterpillar?
Are you looking for something to eat?
Your "woolly bear" won't find anything
to eat on your arm.

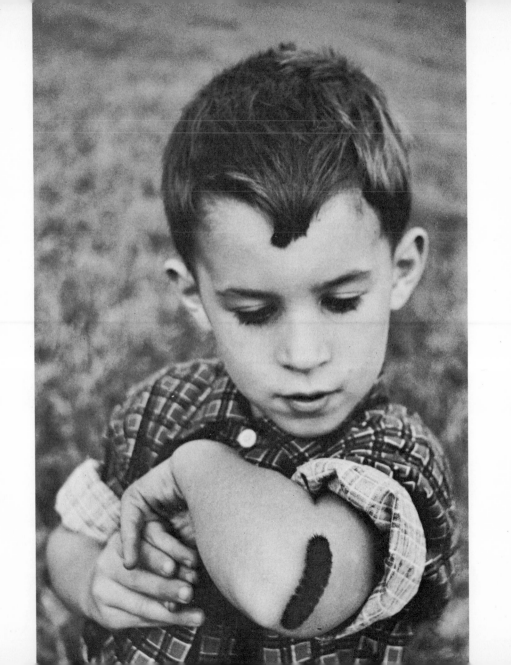

Have you seen a leaf that looks like this
growing on your lawn?
It's a plantain leaf.
This is the kind of leaf
woolly bear caterpillars eat.

Do you want to feed your caterpillar?
Put him in a jar
with a little dirt at the bottom.
He'll be safe there while you are finding
some plantain leaves.

Don't expect your caterpillar
to eat right away.
He may not be hungry.
Leave him for a little while
and when you come back,
look carefully in your jar.
If you see some holes in the leaves,
you'll know your caterpillar
was hungry, after all.
When you have time,
take your caterpillar out of the jar
and let him crawl around on your hand.

87

Count his legs.

Did you count up to six?

Your caterpillar has six little legs.

But he isn't hanging on to your fingers
with those legs, is he?

He is hanging on with his prolegs.

They are not real legs,
but they help him to move along, just the same.

See his mouth and his two black eyes.

He looks scary when you see him so close.

Are you getting tired
of having your caterpillar around?
Then it is time
to take him out of doors again.
Put him on the ground
and let him crawl away.
He will find a good place to sleep
for the winter.
Good-by "woolly bear"

The colder it grows outside,

the harder it is to find things to catch.

Many little creatures have already started

their deep sleep in some snug hiding place.

Winter is here.

But you know that after a while
the snows of winter will melt,
and the air will begin to grow warm again.
Spring and summer will come once more.
A spring and summer filled with
butterflies and ladybugs,
polliwogs and snails,
beetles and darning needles . . .
You'd better save some jars.
You'll need them
when you go out catching again!